SORRY
YOU'RE DATING
AN
A**HOLE!

"I'M SORRY YOU'RE DATING AN ASSHOLE,
THE KIND YOU SWIPED RIGHT ON DURING A SCROLL.

HE SLID IN YOUR DMS WITH A PIC WAY TOO BOLD,
'HEY BABE, LIKE WHAT YOU SEE?' (SO CRINGEY, SO COLD).

WEDDING BELLS? PRETTY FLOWER, HE'S BARELY A RING TONE—
TIME TO DITCH THIS JERK; IT'S BETTER BEING ALONE."

CHEAP

"YOU KNEW HE WAS CHEAP FROM THE VERY START,
ALWAYS 'FORGETTING' HIS WALLET (WHAT A SWEETHEART!).

SUGGESTING YOU SPLIT EVERY BURGER AND FRY,
TREATING YOU LIKE A ROOMMATE—WHAT A PUSSY GUY.

HE NEVER PLANS DATES, SAYS HE'S 'JUST A BAD PLANNER,'
BUT HE CAN ALWAYS PLAN FOR A LATE-NIGHT, 'COME-OVER' MANNER.

HE TALKS BIG ABOUT ALL THE PLACES HE'LL TAKE YOU TO,
BUT, PRETTY FLOWER, HE NEVER FOLLOWS THROUGH."

NOT THAT ATTRACTIVE

"LOOKS AREN'T EVERYTHING, BUT LET'S BE REAL,
WE LIKE OUR MEN TALL AND HOT, IT'S THE DEAL.

IF HE'S NOT TALL OR HOT, HE BETTER GO ALL OUT,
WITH GRAND GESTURES, SURPRISES—SHOWING LOVE, NO DOUBT.

IF HE'S MISSING IN HEIGHT, HE BETTER MAKE UP IN PAY,
WHY SETTLE FOR CRUMBS WHEN YOU DESERVE A GOOD LAY?"

SINGLE FOR A LONG TIME

"SINGLE FOR AGES—DIDN'T YOU SEE THE SIGNS?
HE'S AT BARS EVERY NIGHT, LEAVING HIS EX AND KIDS BEHIND.

THE GOOD ONES GET SNAPPED UP, ADDED TO THE FAMILY TREE,
BUT HE'S STILL OUT THERE, ROAMING WILD AND FREE.

IF HE'S GOT EXCUSES AND ZERO CHIVALRY TO USE,
PRETTY FLOWER, IT'S TIME TO CUT HIM THE F*** LOOSE!"

Not That Great in Bed

"He's a one-minute wonder, over before it began,
It took you longer to undress than it took for this man.

Not a single orgasm, and he doesn't care,
Leaves you high and dry while he snoozes in there.

So now you go home, grab your trusty toy,
Because he's more 'quick exit' than 'bring the joy.'

You can't possibly think this man is the one—
You've had sex ten times, and he's never made you cum."

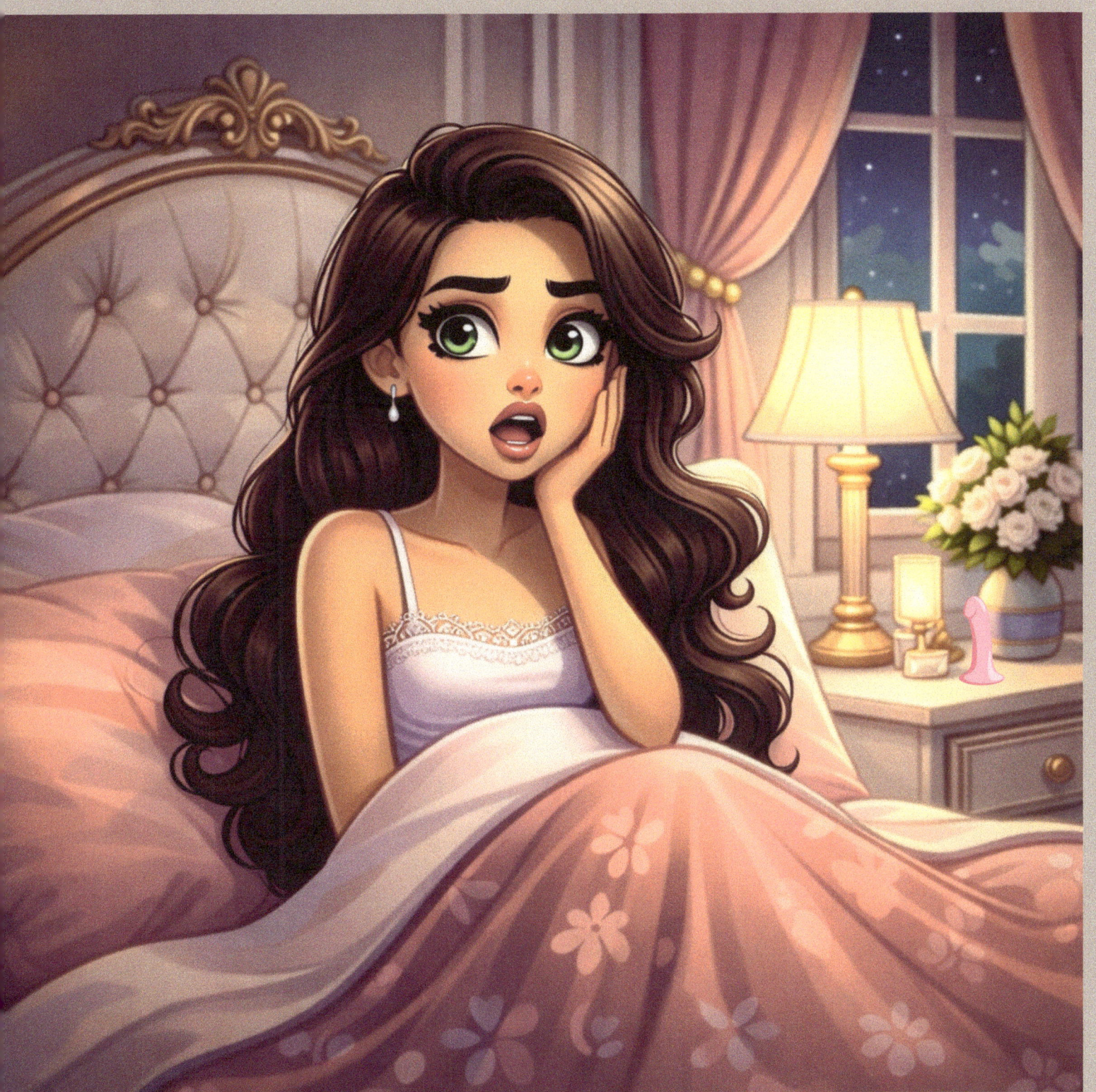

What's His Job?

"A 'JOB' WAS A MYSTERY, ONE HE'D EXPLORE,
YET SOMEHOW HIS TITLE IS STILL 'BETWEEN MORE.'

CAN YOU REALLY MARRY A MAN MAKING PENNIES A DAY,
DO YOU WANT TO PAY ALIMONY EVERY PAYDAY?

WHEN HE DOES WORK, IT'S A HALF-BAKED SCHEME,
SELLING NFTS OR 'REPPING' A DREAM.

YOU'RE HUSTLING HARD WHILE HE'S GAMING AWAY—
SERIOUSLY, WHY ARE YOU DATING THIS STRAY?"

SPLITTER

"HE HAS YOU SPLITTING EVERYTHING OR PAYING IT ALL,
THIS MAN HAS NO MONEY—AND HE'S NOT EVEN TALL.

HE'S NOT INTO CHIVALRY BUT WANTS HIS CAKE AND EAT IT TOO—
WHY ARE YOU DATING HIM? WHAT'S WRONG WITH YOU?

YOU DIDN'T SIGN UP FOR THIS POOR, SAD MATCH—
ARE YOU REALLY THAT DESPERATE, DATING A MAN WHO'S NO CATCH?"

NOT SMART

"HE'S NOT FUN TO TALK TO, HE'S NOT THAT BRIGHT,
NEEDS CHATGPT FOR KIDS' TRIVIA NIGHT.

HE'S KINDA CUTE, BUT THAT CAN'T MAKE UP FOR DUMB—
YOU AND I BOTH KNOW THAT GUY'S NOT THE ONE.

I CARE ABOUT YOU, SO SORRY TO VENT,
BUT WHY ARE YOU DATING A LOSER WHO'S NOT INTELLIGENT?"

STUPID GIFTS

"His gifts come from the dollar store,
plastic roses for Valentine's—but who's keeping score?

An Irish friendship ring though you're clearly Persian,
and somehow you paid for every excursion.

His thoughtlessness is sucking your soul,
I really need you to explain why you're dating an asshole."

PHONE ADDICTION

"HE'S GLUED TO HIS PHONE, DOESN'T PAY MUCH ATTENTION TO YOU.
HE EVEN LOOKS AT IT WHILE HE'S INSIDE OF YOU.

OUT TO DINNER? HE'S SCROLLING AWAY,
THEN YOU KNOW THE DRILL—EXPECTS YOU TO PAY.

IF HIS PHONE'S GETTING HIM OFF MORE THAN YOU,
TRADE HIM IN FAST FOR A BETTER SCREW!"

MOMMY ISSUES

"HE CALLS AND TEXTS HIS MOM AFTER EVERYTHING YOU DO,
IT'S CLEAR SHE'S THE LOVE OF HIS LIFE—IT'S TRUE.

SHE STILL DOES HIS LAUNDRY, STILL COOKS HIS MEALS,
TO HER, HE'S A PRINCE, AND YOU'RE JUST THE THIRD WHEEL.

HOW MANY RED FLAGS DO YOU NEED TO SEE,
BEFORE YOU FINALLY DUMP THIS MAMA'S BOY AND BREAK FREE?"

THANKSGIVING

He invited his ex for Thanksgiving, not you,
Are you really that clueless, without a single clue?

When a man loves a woman, he's by her side,
Not off with an ex, leaving her pride denied.

Are you as dumb as stuffing or clueless as turkey?
He's feeding you lies, keeping things murky.

CHRISTMAS

YOU FORGAVE THANKSGIVING, WHAT CAN I SAY,
YOU'RE CLUELESS, PRETTY FLOWER, IN SUCH DISARRAY.

NOW IT'S CHRISTMAS, HIS FAMILY ALL NEAR,
AND GUESS WHO'S THERE—YEP, HEATHER THE EX, MY DEAR!

SO THICK, EVEN SANTA'S CALLING IT QUITS,
YOU'RE ON THE NAUGHTY LIST FOR CLUELESSNESS, TWITS!

BIRTHDAY

OH, IT'S YOUR BIRTHDAY, AND GUESS WHO'S AWAY,
HE'LL "MAKE IT UP LATER," YEAH, SURE, OKAY.

MEN LOVE YOUNGER WOMEN; YOU'RE GETTING SO OLD,
YOU'RE GOING TO DIE ALONE, LET THE TRUTH BE TOLD.

ANOTHER YEAR OLDER, ALONE AS CAN BE,
MIGHT AS WELL START KNITTING FOR YOUR "ONE CAT" FAMILY.

THE END

MAKE YOUR CHOICE, BUT HERE'S MY ADVICE,
STICK WITH AN A**HOLE, AND YOU'LL PAY THE PRICE.

YOU'LL END UP ALONE, TRYING TO PRETEND,
BUT THAT'S NOT WHAT YOU WANT—JUST A CRAPPY END.

HE'LL MOVE ON FAST, HE'S THAT KIND OF GUY,
SOME DESPERATE WOMAN WILL MARRY HIM, NO LIE.

SO MOVE ON NOW, BEFORE YOU END UP SOLO,
WITH A CAT BY YOUR SIDE, NAMED AFTER SHOES—MANOLO.

LOVE ALWAYS FINDS YOU
WHEN YOU LEAST EXPECT IT!
STAY HAPPY & SINGLE UNTIL THEN!

(DON'T DATE AN A**HOLE!)